In the Deep and Dark

Felicia Jowett

BookLeaf Publishing

Presentation by *BookLeaf Publishing*

Web: www.bookleafpub.com

E-mail: info@bookleafpub.com

ISBN: 9789357444729

First edition 2022

You

The sweet curve of your smile
drives me to distraction.
Your careful touch
lights me up inside.
In the dark I
pretend that I can feel
your eyes on me.
The weight of your gaze
sends a thrill through me.
And I am left wanting.

Caught

Soundlessly screaming
into the night,
these ghosts haunt me.
These memories
like chains,
keep me locked up tight.
These whispers
sink into my mind,
my darkest thoughts trapped.

Darling Dear

The words always come easiest
After I've seen your face
When the day is done
And night settles in

When I'm alone with nothing
But my thoughts
And the memory
Of your hand in mine

Kiss

I keep thinking of that kiss;
the way his hand gripped your waist
the way there was no space
between your bodies.

Transfixed, my breath caught
and my skin went hot
stunned and in awe that you
would let me see this.

Regrets

You have never touched me...

But I remember your eyes, your leer.

I recall the comments you made.

The pictures you took.

The way I thought I was crazy.

How I made sure we were never alone.

How I kept it a secret.

Years later it makes me cringe.

And I hate myself for staying silent.

The First

There is something lovely
about the way
new leaves in spring unfurl.
That reminds me of the way
you touched me
fingers gentle, wondrous feeling.

May 5th

In the dark I feel you near me
And I miss you more than I can say
I see your face in my dreams
I still hear your voice
In the strings of this old guitar

This hole of grief expands in my chest
And rest does not come easy
My heart is heavy, beating slow
Sinking under the weight
Drowning in these memories

Crave

Your touch is a brand upon my skin
Burning deeply though unseen
I crave the way you hold me
The way you pull me close and tight

Keep me in your arms a little longer
I'm not willing to let you go
Let me curl against your chest
Inhale exhale towards sleep

Autumn

The turning of the wheel
Days growing shorter
Crisp frost beneath my feet

Breathing in chilled air
Exhaling white smoke
Clear skies high above me

Leaves begin their descent
Swirling to the ground below
Branches bare against white clouds

A new season dawns

Childhood

The park I used to play in
The streets I used to run
Curfew was the streetlights
A chorus of goodbyes

Summertime sun rose early
Morning swims in stifling heat
Bike rides through quiet streets
Crickets slip between our fingers

Play pretend and make believe
From swings we touched the sky
Hide and seek behind the bush
Laughter echoing off concrete walls

Drift

Steady
Are your hands
That hold me

Breath
A soothing
Counterpart to mine

Heartbeat
An even thump
Drumming in my ear

Connection

blazing heat above
cool moisture below

calm within
fire without

feet buried in sand
in dry dirt
in water

Promise

a connection, a thread, a rope
a binding everlasting

hope is a light though I
cling to darkness
the brightness will find me

points on a compass to guide me
the stars will lead me home
the moon will light my path

I will find you within me

Under

I miss the way
You made me feel
A dreamy haze
Your slow embrace
The way you made
My limbs hang heavy
And everything else
Began to fade

To You

It doesn't matter
Where you
To get to you
I'll map the stars

Mercy

You forgive too easily
Your heart on your sleeve
For those who don't deserve

Your mercy is a gift
A soothing balm
Do not give it lightly

Heart

You say this soft heart
Is a weakness
But I say
That this heart
Is my greatest asset

Dream

In the blue light
Of the full moon
You are ethereal

Beautiful
A distant dream
A waking dream

A secret to be kept

June 1st

Today
I caught a scent
That I haven't
Smelled in years

The musk of your cologne
Brought tears to my eyes
And a rush of memories
I thought I'd forgotten

(the memory of my first sleep away camp, your
cologne on pillow so I wouldn't be homesick;
the nights you got dressed up to go out, that
scent is wound through all my childhood
memories)

Growth

Under the light
Of a gibbous moon
I feel gratitude for
All the seeds I've planted
And the way that I
Have grown reaching
Towards new life

A.E.K

Little one,
You are sorely missed
But deeply loved.

Your brief presence
On earth with us
Short but sweet

Dear one,
We will meet again
My little angel

www.ingramcontent.com/pod-product-compliance
Lightning Source LLC
LaVergne TN
LVHW050310200726

843509LV00015B/3255